50 Flavored Butter for Home Cooking Recipes

By: Kelly Johnson

Table of Contents

- Garlic Herb Butter
- Lemon Dill Butter
- Honey Cinnamon Butter
- Roasted Red Pepper Butter
- Chive and Onion Butter
- Sriracha Lime Butter
- Basil Pesto Butter
- Smoky Chipotle Butter
- Maple Bacon Butter
- Truffle Parmesan Butter
- Sun-Dried Tomato Butter
- Cranberry Orange Butter
- Jalapeño Lime Butter
- Rosemary Garlic Butter
- Blueberry Honey Butter
- Tarragon Mustard Butter
- Brown Sugar Bourbon Butter
- Wasabi Sesame Butter
- Curry Coconut Butter
- Cilantro Lime Butter
- Blackberry Sage Butter
- Smoky Paprika Butter
- Mint Chocolate Butter
- Horseradish Dill Butter
- Cajun Spice Butter
- Pineapple Rum Butter
- Apple Cinnamon Butter
- Lavender Honey Butter
- Espresso Cocoa Butter
- Sweet Chili Lime Butter
- Pistachio Rose Butter
- Pumpkin Spice Butter
- Spicy Mango Butter
- Black Garlic Butter
- Chimichurri Butter
- Hibiscus Honey Butter

- Roasted Garlic Lemon Butter
- Apricot Basil Butter
- Thai Peanut Butter
- Lemon Pepper Butter
- Raspberry Balsamic Butter
- Fig Walnut Butter
- Caramel Apple Butter
- Herb Feta Butter
- Ginger Lime Butter
- Smoked Salmon Dill Butter
- Cumin Coriander Butter
- Cranberry Sage Butter
- Maple Almond Butter
- Zesty Orange Butter

Garlic Herb Butter

Ingredients:

- 1 cup (2 sticks) unsalted butter, softened
- 4 cloves garlic, minced
- 2 tablespoons fresh parsley, chopped
- 1 tablespoon fresh thyme leaves, chopped
- 1 tablespoon fresh rosemary, chopped
- 1 tablespoon fresh chives, chopped (optional)
- 1/2 teaspoon salt (adjust to taste)
- 1/4 teaspoon black pepper

Instructions:

1. **Prep the Butter**: In a medium bowl, add the softened butter.
2. **Add Herbs and Garlic**: Add the minced garlic, chopped parsley, thyme, rosemary, chives (if using), salt, and pepper.
3. **Mix**: Use a fork or a spoon to mix everything together until well-combined.
4. **Shape**: Transfer the mixture to a sheet of parchment paper or plastic wrap. Roll it into a log shape, twisting the ends to seal.
5. **Chill**: Place in the refrigerator for at least 1 hour, until firm.
6. **Serve**: Slice and enjoy on bread, meat, or veggies!

Storage: Keeps for up to 1 week in the fridge or up to 3 months in the freezer.

Lemon Dill Butter

Ingredients:

- 1 cup (2 sticks) unsalted butter, softened
- Zest of 1 lemon
- 1 tablespoon lemon juice
- 2 tablespoons fresh dill, chopped
- 1/2 teaspoon salt (adjust to taste)

Instructions:

1. In a medium bowl, combine the softened butter, lemon zest, lemon juice, chopped dill, and salt.
2. Mix until well-combined.
3. Shape into a log on parchment paper, wrap, and chill for at least 1 hour before serving.

Honey Cinnamon Butter

Ingredients:

- 1 cup (2 sticks) unsalted butter, softened
- 3 tablespoons honey
- 1 teaspoon ground cinnamon
- 1/4 teaspoon salt

Instructions:

1. In a medium bowl, mix the softened butter with honey, cinnamon, and salt.
2. Stir until smooth and creamy.
3. Transfer to a container or shape into a log and refrigerate for 1 hour to firm up.

Roasted Red Pepper Butter

Ingredients:

- 1 cup (2 sticks) unsalted butter, softened
- 1/4 cup roasted red peppers, finely chopped
- 1 clove garlic, minced
- 1/2 teaspoon smoked paprika
- 1/2 teaspoon salt

Instructions:

1. In a medium bowl, combine the softened butter, roasted red peppers, garlic, smoked paprika, and salt.
2. Stir until fully mixed and smooth.
3. Place on parchment paper, roll into a log, and refrigerate for at least 1 hour before serving.

Chive and Onion Butter

Ingredients:

- 1 cup (2 sticks) unsalted butter, softened
- 2 tablespoons fresh chives, chopped
- 1 tablespoon onion, finely chopped (or onion powder to taste)
- 1/2 teaspoon salt

Instructions:

1. In a medium bowl, mix the softened butter with chives, onion, and salt until well combined.
2. Shape into a log, wrap in parchment paper, and chill for at least 1 hour before serving.

Sriracha Lime Butter

Ingredients:

- 1 cup (2 sticks) unsalted butter, softened
- 2 tablespoons Sriracha sauce
- Zest of 1 lime
- 1 tablespoon lime juice
- 1/4 teaspoon salt

Instructions:

1. In a medium bowl, combine the softened butter, Sriracha, lime zest, lime juice, and salt.
2. Mix until smooth and well blended.
3. Transfer to parchment paper, shape into a log, and refrigerate for at least 1 hour before serving.

Basil Pesto Butter

Ingredients:

- 1 cup (2 sticks) unsalted butter, softened
- 1/4 cup basil pesto
- 1/2 teaspoon salt

Instructions:

1. In a medium bowl, mix the softened butter with basil pesto and salt until fully incorporated.
2. Shape into a log, wrap in parchment paper, and chill for at least 1 hour before serving.

Smoky Chipotle Butter

Ingredients:

- 1 cup (2 sticks) unsalted butter, softened
- 1-2 tablespoons chipotle in adobo sauce, finely chopped
- 1/2 teaspoon smoked paprika
- 1/2 teaspoon salt

Instructions:

1. In a medium bowl, combine the softened butter, chipotle, smoked paprika, and salt.
2. Mix until well combined and smooth.
3. Roll into a log using parchment paper and refrigerate for at least 1 hour before serving.

Maple Bacon Butter

Ingredients:

- 1 cup (2 sticks) unsalted butter, softened
- 1/4 cup cooked bacon, crumbled
- 2 tablespoons maple syrup
- 1/2 teaspoon salt

Instructions:

1. In a medium bowl, mix the softened butter with crumbled bacon, maple syrup, and salt until well combined.
2. Shape into a log, wrap in parchment paper, and chill for at least 1 hour before serving.

Truffle Parmesan Butter

Ingredients:

- 1 cup (2 sticks) unsalted butter, softened
- 2 tablespoons truffle oil
- 1/4 cup grated Parmesan cheese
- 1/2 teaspoon salt

Instructions:

1. In a medium bowl, combine the softened butter, truffle oil, grated Parmesan, and salt.
2. Mix until smooth and well blended.
3. Shape into a log, wrap in parchment paper, and chill for at least 1 hour before serving.

Sun-Dried Tomato Butter

Ingredients:

- 1 cup (2 sticks) unsalted butter, softened
- 1/4 cup sun-dried tomatoes, finely chopped
- 1 tablespoon fresh basil, chopped
- 1/2 teaspoon garlic powder
- 1/2 teaspoon salt

Instructions:

1. In a medium bowl, mix the softened butter with sun-dried tomatoes, basil, garlic powder, and salt until fully incorporated.
2. Shape into a log, wrap in parchment paper, and refrigerate for at least 1 hour before serving.

Cranberry Orange Butter

Ingredients:

- 1 cup (2 sticks) unsalted butter, softened
- 1/4 cup dried cranberries, finely chopped
- Zest of 1 orange
- 1 tablespoon orange juice
- 1/2 teaspoon salt

Instructions:

1. In a medium bowl, combine the softened butter, cranberries, orange zest, orange juice, and salt.
2. Mix until well combined.
3. Shape into a log, wrap in parchment paper, and chill for at least 1 hour before serving.

Jalapeño Lime Butter

Ingredients:

- 1 cup (2 sticks) unsalted butter, softened
- 1-2 jalapeños, seeded and finely chopped
- Zest of 1 lime
- 1 tablespoon lime juice
- 1/2 teaspoon salt

Instructions:

1. In a medium bowl, mix the softened butter with jalapeños, lime zest, lime juice, and salt until well combined.
2. Shape into a log, wrap in parchment paper, and chill for at least 1 hour before serving.

Rosemary Garlic Butter

Ingredients:

- 1 cup (2 sticks) unsalted butter, softened
- 2-3 cloves garlic, minced
- 2 tablespoons fresh rosemary, chopped
- 1/2 teaspoon salt

Instructions:

1. In a medium bowl, combine the softened butter, minced garlic, chopped rosemary, and salt.
2. Mix until fully blended and smooth.
3. Roll into a log using parchment paper and refrigerate for at least 1 hour before serving.

Blueberry Honey Butter

Ingredients:

- 1 cup (2 sticks) unsalted butter, softened
- 1/4 cup fresh or frozen blueberries, mashed
- 3 tablespoons honey
- 1/4 teaspoon salt

Instructions:

1. In a medium bowl, mix the softened butter with mashed blueberries, honey, and salt until well combined.
2. Shape into a log, wrap in parchment paper, and chill for at least 1 hour before serving.

Tarragon Mustard Butter

Ingredients:

- 1 cup (2 sticks) unsalted butter, softened
- 2 tablespoons Dijon mustard
- 1 tablespoon fresh tarragon, chopped
- 1/2 teaspoon salt

Instructions:

1. In a medium bowl, combine the softened butter, Dijon mustard, chopped tarragon, and salt.
2. Mix until smooth and fully incorporated.
3. Shape into a log, wrap in parchment paper, and refrigerate for at least 1 hour before serving.

Brown Sugar Bourbon Butter

Ingredients:

- 1 cup (2 sticks) unsalted butter, softened
- 1/4 cup brown sugar, packed
- 2 tablespoons bourbon
- 1/2 teaspoon vanilla extract
- 1/4 teaspoon salt

Instructions:

1. In a medium bowl, mix the softened butter with brown sugar, bourbon, vanilla extract, and salt until smooth.
2. Shape into a log, wrap in parchment paper, and chill for at least 1 hour before serving.

Wasabi Sesame Butter

Ingredients:

- 1 cup (2 sticks) unsalted butter, softened
- 1-2 teaspoons wasabi paste (adjust to taste)
- 1 tablespoon toasted sesame oil
- 1 tablespoon sesame seeds
- 1/2 teaspoon salt

Instructions:

1. In a medium bowl, combine the softened butter, wasabi paste, sesame oil, sesame seeds, and salt.
2. Mix until well blended.
3. Roll into a log using parchment paper and refrigerate for at least 1 hour before serving.

Curry Coconut Butter

Ingredients:

- 1 cup (2 sticks) unsalted butter, softened
- 2 tablespoons coconut milk
- 2 teaspoons curry powder
- 1/2 teaspoon salt

Instructions:

1. In a medium bowl, mix the softened butter with coconut milk, curry powder, and salt until fully incorporated.
2. Shape into a log, wrap in parchment paper, and chill for at least 1 hour before serving.

Cilantro Lime Butter

Ingredients:

- 1 cup (2 sticks) unsalted butter, softened
- 2 tablespoons fresh cilantro, chopped
- Zest of 1 lime
- 1 tablespoon lime juice
- 1/2 teaspoon salt

Instructions:

1. In a medium bowl, combine the softened butter, chopped cilantro, lime zest, lime juice, and salt.
2. Mix until well combined and smooth.
3. Roll into a log using parchment paper and refrigerate for at least 1 hour before serving.

Blackberry Sage Butter

Ingredients:

- 1 cup (2 sticks) unsalted butter, softened
- 1/4 cup fresh blackberries, mashed
- 1 tablespoon fresh sage, chopped
- 1/4 teaspoon salt

Instructions:

1. In a medium bowl, mix the softened butter with mashed blackberries, chopped sage, and salt until well combined.
2. Shape into a log, wrap in parchment paper, and chill for at least 1 hour before serving.

Smoky Paprika Butter

Ingredients:

- 1 cup (2 sticks) unsalted butter, softened
- 2 teaspoons smoked paprika
- 1 clove garlic, minced
- 1/2 teaspoon salt

Instructions:

1. In a medium bowl, combine the softened butter, smoked paprika, minced garlic, and salt.
2. Mix until fully blended and smooth.
3. Roll into a log using parchment paper and refrigerate for at least 1 hour before serving.

Mint Chocolate Butter

Ingredients:

- 1 cup (2 sticks) unsalted butter, softened
- 3 tablespoons cocoa powder
- 1 tablespoon peppermint extract
- 1/4 cup powdered sugar
- 1/4 teaspoon salt

Instructions:

1. In a medium bowl, mix the softened butter with cocoa powder, peppermint extract, powdered sugar, and salt until smooth.
2. Shape into a log, wrap in parchment paper, and chill for at least 1 hour before serving.

Horseradish Dill Butter

Ingredients:

- 1 cup (2 sticks) unsalted butter, softened
- 2 tablespoons prepared horseradish
- 2 tablespoons fresh dill, chopped
- 1/2 teaspoon salt

Instructions:

1. In a medium bowl, combine the softened butter, horseradish, chopped dill, and salt.
2. Mix until well combined.
3. Roll into a log using parchment paper and refrigerate for at least 1 hour before serving.

Cajun Spice Butter

Ingredients:

- 1 cup (2 sticks) unsalted butter, softened
- 1 tablespoon Cajun seasoning
- 1/2 teaspoon garlic powder
- 1/2 teaspoon salt

Instructions:

1. In a medium bowl, mix the softened butter with Cajun seasoning, garlic powder, and salt until fully incorporated.
2. Shape into a log, wrap in parchment paper, and chill for at least 1 hour before serving.

Pineapple Rum Butter

Ingredients:

- 1 cup (2 sticks) unsalted butter, softened
- 1/4 cup crushed pineapple, drained
- 2 tablespoons dark rum
- 1/4 teaspoon salt

Instructions:

1. In a medium bowl, mix the softened butter with crushed pineapple, dark rum, and salt until smooth and well combined.
2. Shape into a log, wrap in parchment paper, and chill for at least 1 hour before serving.

Apple Cinnamon Butter

Ingredients:

- 1 cup (2 sticks) unsalted butter, softened
- 1/4 cup applesauce
- 2 teaspoons ground cinnamon
- 1/4 teaspoon salt

Instructions:

1. In a medium bowl, combine the softened butter, applesauce, cinnamon, and salt.
2. Mix until fully blended and smooth.
3. Roll into a log using parchment paper and refrigerate for at least 1 hour before serving.

Lavender Honey Butter

Ingredients:

- 1 cup (2 sticks) unsalted butter, softened
- 2 tablespoons honey
- 1 tablespoon dried culinary lavender
- 1/4 teaspoon salt

Instructions:

1. In a medium bowl, mix the softened butter with honey, dried lavender, and salt until well combined.
2. Shape into a log, wrap in parchment paper, and chill for at least 1 hour before serving.

Espresso Cocoa Butter

Ingredients:

- 1 cup (2 sticks) unsalted butter, softened
- 2 tablespoons cocoa powder
- 1 tablespoon instant espresso powder
- 1/4 cup powdered sugar
- 1/4 teaspoon salt

Instructions:

1. In a medium bowl, mix the softened butter with cocoa powder, espresso powder, powdered sugar, and salt until smooth and well combined.
2. Shape into a log, wrap in parchment paper, and chill for at least 1 hour before serving.

Sweet Chili Lime Butter

Ingredients:

- 1 cup (2 sticks) unsalted butter, softened
- 2 tablespoons sweet chili sauce
- Zest of 1 lime
- 1 tablespoon lime juice
- 1/2 teaspoon salt

Instructions:

1. In a medium bowl, combine the softened butter with sweet chili sauce, lime zest, lime juice, and salt.
2. Mix until fully blended and smooth.
3. Roll into a log using parchment paper and refrigerate for at least 1 hour before serving.

Pistachio Rose Butter

Ingredients:

- 1 cup (2 sticks) unsalted butter, softened
- 1/2 cup pistachios, finely chopped
- 1 tablespoon rose water
- 1/4 teaspoon salt

Instructions:

1. In a medium bowl, mix the softened butter with chopped pistachios, rose water, and salt until well combined.
2. Shape into a log, wrap in parchment paper, and chill for at least 1 hour before serving.

Pumpkin Spice Butter

Ingredients:

- 1 cup (2 sticks) unsalted butter, softened
- 1/4 cup pumpkin puree
- 2 teaspoons pumpkin pie spice
- 1/4 teaspoon salt

Instructions:

1. In a medium bowl, combine the softened butter with pumpkin puree, pumpkin pie spice, and salt.
2. Mix until smooth and fully incorporated.
3. Roll into a log using parchment paper and refrigerate for at least 1 hour before serving.

Spicy Mango Butter

Ingredients:

- 1 cup (2 sticks) unsalted butter, softened
- 1/4 cup mango puree
- 1-2 teaspoons chili powder (adjust to taste)
- 1/2 teaspoon salt

Instructions:

1. In a medium bowl, mix the softened butter with mango puree, chili powder, and salt until well combined.
2. Shape into a log, wrap in parchment paper, and chill for at least 1 hour before serving.

Black Garlic Butter

Ingredients:

- 1 cup (2 sticks) unsalted butter, softened
- 4-5 cloves black garlic, mashed
- 1/2 teaspoon salt

Instructions:

1. In a medium bowl, combine the softened butter with mashed black garlic and salt.
2. Mix until smooth and fully incorporated.
3. Roll into a log using parchment paper and refrigerate for at least 1 hour before serving.

Chimichurri Butter

Ingredients:

- 1 cup (2 sticks) unsalted butter, softened
- 1/4 cup chimichurri sauce (store-bought or homemade)
- 1/4 teaspoon salt

Instructions:

1. In a medium bowl, mix the softened butter with chimichurri sauce and salt until fully combined.
2. Shape into a log, wrap in parchment paper, and chill for at least 1 hour before serving.

Hibiscus Honey Butter

Ingredients:

- 1 cup (2 sticks) unsalted butter, softened
- 2 tablespoons dried hibiscus flowers, finely crushed
- 2 tablespoons honey
- 1/4 teaspoon salt

Instructions:

1. In a medium bowl, mix the softened butter with crushed hibiscus flowers, honey, and salt until well combined.
2. Shape into a log, wrap in parchment paper, and chill for at least 1 hour before serving.

Roasted Garlic Lemon Butter

Ingredients:

- 1 cup (2 sticks) unsalted butter, softened
- 1 head of garlic, roasted
- Zest of 1 lemon
- 1 tablespoon lemon juice
- 1/4 teaspoon salt

Instructions:

1. Squeeze the roasted garlic cloves out of their skins and mash them in a bowl.
2. Combine the mashed garlic with the softened butter, lemon zest, lemon juice, and salt.
3. Mix until well blended and smooth.
4. Shape into a log, wrap in parchment paper, and chill for at least 1 hour before serving.

Apricot Basil Butter

Ingredients:

- 1 cup (2 sticks) unsalted butter, softened
- 1/4 cup dried apricots, finely chopped
- 2 tablespoons fresh basil, chopped
- 1/4 teaspoon salt

Instructions:

1. In a medium bowl, combine the softened butter with chopped apricots, chopped basil, and salt.
2. Mix until fully incorporated.
3. Roll into a log using parchment paper and refrigerate for at least 1 hour before serving.

Thai Peanut Butter

Ingredients:

- 1 cup (2 sticks) unsalted butter, softened
- 1/4 cup creamy peanut butter
- 2 tablespoons soy sauce
- 1 tablespoon lime juice
- 1/2 teaspoon chili flakes (adjust to taste)

Instructions:

1. In a medium bowl, mix the softened butter with peanut butter, soy sauce, lime juice, and chili flakes until smooth and well combined.
2. Shape into a log, wrap in parchment paper, and chill for at least 1 hour before serving.

Lemon Pepper Butter

Ingredients:

- 1 cup (2 sticks) unsalted butter, softened
- 1 tablespoon lemon zest
- 1 teaspoon freshly ground black pepper
- 1/2 teaspoon salt

Instructions:

1. In a medium bowl, combine the softened butter with lemon zest, black pepper, and salt.
2. Mix until fully blended and smooth.
3. Roll into a log using parchment paper and refrigerate for at least 1 hour before serving.

Raspberry Balsamic Butter

Ingredients:

- 1 cup (2 sticks) unsalted butter, softened
- 1/4 cup fresh raspberries, mashed
- 2 tablespoons balsamic vinegar
- 1/4 teaspoon salt

Instructions:

1. In a medium bowl, mix the softened butter with mashed raspberries, balsamic vinegar, and salt until well combined.
2. Shape into a log, wrap in parchment paper, and chill for at least 1 hour before serving.

Fig Walnut Butter

Ingredients:

- 1 cup (2 sticks) unsalted butter, softened
- 1/4 cup dried figs, finely chopped
- 1/4 cup walnuts, toasted and chopped
- 1/4 teaspoon salt

Instructions:

1. In a medium bowl, combine the softened butter with chopped figs, walnuts, and salt.
2. Mix until fully incorporated.
3. Roll into a log using parchment paper and refrigerate for at least 1 hour before serving.

Caramel Apple Butter

Ingredients:

- 1 cup (2 sticks) unsalted butter, softened
- 1/4 cup apple cider
- 2 tablespoons caramel sauce
- 1/2 teaspoon cinnamon
- 1/4 teaspoon salt

Instructions:

1. In a medium bowl, mix the softened butter with apple cider, caramel sauce, cinnamon, and salt until smooth and well blended.
2. Shape into a log, wrap in parchment paper, and chill for at least 1 hour before serving.

Herb Feta Butter

Ingredients:

- 1 cup (2 sticks) unsalted butter, softened
- 1/4 cup crumbled feta cheese
- 2 tablespoons fresh herbs (such as parsley, chives, or dill), chopped
- 1/4 teaspoon salt

Instructions:

1. In a medium bowl, combine the softened butter with crumbled feta, chopped herbs, and salt.
2. Mix until well combined.
3. Roll into a log using parchment paper and refrigerate for at least 1 hour before serving.

Ginger Lime Butter

Ingredients:

- 1 cup (2 sticks) unsalted butter, softened
- 1 tablespoon fresh ginger, grated
- Zest of 1 lime
- 1 tablespoon lime juice
- 1/4 teaspoon salt

Instructions:

1. In a medium bowl, combine the softened butter with grated ginger, lime zest, lime juice, and salt.
2. Mix until well blended and smooth.
3. Shape into a log, wrap in parchment paper, and chill for at least 1 hour before serving.

Smoked Salmon Dill Butter

Ingredients:

- 1 cup (2 sticks) unsalted butter, softened
- 1/4 cup smoked salmon, finely chopped
- 2 tablespoons fresh dill, chopped
- 1 teaspoon lemon juice
- 1/4 teaspoon salt

Instructions:

1. In a medium bowl, mix the softened butter with chopped smoked salmon, dill, lemon juice, and salt until fully incorporated.
2. Roll into a log using parchment paper and refrigerate for at least 1 hour before serving.

Cumin Coriander Butter

Ingredients:

- 1 cup (2 sticks) unsalted butter, softened
- 1 teaspoon ground cumin
- 1 teaspoon ground coriander
- 1 tablespoon fresh cilantro, chopped
- 1/4 teaspoon salt

Instructions:

1. In a medium bowl, combine the softened butter with ground cumin, ground coriander, chopped cilantro, and salt.
2. Mix until well blended and smooth.
3. Shape into a log, wrap in parchment paper, and chill for at least 1 hour before serving.

Cranberry Sage Butter

Ingredients:

- 1 cup (2 sticks) unsalted butter, softened
- 1/2 cup dried cranberries, finely chopped
- 1 tablespoon fresh sage, chopped
- 1/4 teaspoon salt

Instructions:

1. In a medium bowl, mix the softened butter with chopped cranberries, chopped sage, and salt until fully combined.
2. Shape into a log, wrap in parchment paper, and chill for at least 1 hour before serving.

Maple Almond Butter

Ingredients:

- 1 cup (2 sticks) unsalted butter, softened
- 1/4 cup almond butter
- 2 tablespoons maple syrup
- 1/4 teaspoon salt

Instructions:

1. In a medium bowl, combine the softened butter with almond butter, maple syrup, and salt.
2. Mix until smooth and well blended.
3. Roll into a log using parchment paper and refrigerate for at least 1 hour before serving.

Zesty Orange Butter

Ingredients:

- 1 cup (2 sticks) unsalted butter, softened
- Zest of 1 orange
- 1 tablespoon orange juice
- 1/2 teaspoon cinnamon
- 1/4 teaspoon salt

Instructions:

1. In a medium bowl, mix the softened butter with orange zest, orange juice, cinnamon, and salt until fully incorporated.
2. Shape into a log, wrap in parchment paper, and chill for at least 1 hour before serving.